Date Due	

↱

MANIFEST;

AND FURTHERMORE

Poems by

WILLIAM BRONK

NORTH POINT PRESS

San Francisco 1987

Cover design by David Bullen

North Point Press
850 Talbot Avenue
Berkeley, California
94706

The arts have something to tell us.
It is not what we wanted to hear;
but we listen.
It is a very private communication.
It becomes our life.

CONTENTS

MANIFEST

3 Winter Vocative

4 What Foot

5 The Search

6 Out There

7 Your Way Too

8 Futurity

9 The House That Doesn't House

10 Endings, the End

11 The Disposition

12 Even Don't

13 Someone Comes By

14 Umpire

15 Certain Questions

16 The Action

17 Something Going On

18 Friends of the Earth

19 Structural Stresses

20 Fort Edward

21 Short Terms

22 A Consolation of Cold

23 The Winter Light

24 Present Not Accounted For

25 Winter Evening

26 Manifest

27 The Informer

28 End of February

29   2 + 2 (= 1?)

30   On Some Lines from Virgil

31   Lucifer

32   Astonishment

33   Sportsmonday

34   The Movie

35   Period Metaphor

36   The Word

37   The Life

38   The Age of Science

39   The Powers of Numbers

42   The I's and Ears of the World

43   How Else?

44   Manner of Speaking

AND FURTHERMORE

47   Aura

48   Plenary Indulgence

49   Nolo Contendere

50   So Long

51   Folly

52   Some Where

53   Mortal Loves

54   The Punchboard

55   The Untold

56   Oxymoronic Fundament

57   Guided Tour

58 Knowledge of Plates

59 Alternative

60 Metaphor Again

61 Outside

62 The Idea of Real

63 Holy Orders

64 Estrangement

65 Anyway

66 For Gil, Coworker

67 Foresight

68 Ruined Place

69 Eating Alone

70 For My Friend, Jerry, He Drunk

71 Stand-by

72 Etiquette

73 Finding the Way

74 Stations

75 The End of the World

76 Getting Older

77 More or Less

MANIFEST

WINTER VOCATIVE

Broken sky-mirror,
blue-shadowed snow,
June is far now,

hold while you can; show
bare of branch
stark of stalk:

ache us to know.

3

WHAT FOOT

We are shoes it wears for the time and then discards.
Nothing wears them again. Memorials,
they show for awhile what foot and where it walked.

THE SEARCH

I want to go to sleep again because
there was something in the dream that seemed right. What?
Something. Oh, there are things we know awake,
too. We won't ever learn what they are about.

OUT THERE

I have laughed with the mind, sometimes hard
and with ugly dismissal, how its last conclusions rot out
initial bases or tight lock up the mind
in a cage it cannot escape from and is held there.

But I accede; knowledge is what I am freed
from, as once I was freed from power, not
having any. Knowledge and power are what
we want until we find, at last, they are not.

There is a state outside of me, too, without
these things. Reality? The God? I apply
to it. It has my reverence and awe, my love.
I am content there where I wanted once.

YOUR WAY TOO

The way Swann, his whole life, loved
Odette and she not even his type, is the way
contrarily, we, each of us, love,
in spite of natural inclinations, our lives.
We trust the tact of others because we know
they know and won't speak of it. Things are far
more complicated than we say they are.

FUTURITY

Not anything I made, not these brief things,
but things I saw about the natural world:
I wish that these could hold there, never be gone.

THE HOUSE THAT DOESN'T HOUSE

I have my own place and live there alone.
In some ways we shape each other perhaps. It's not
the house that lives me though, though something does.

I think of whatever lives us as another house
that we don't have to live in or even know about.
It has space we can go to not to stay
but go home again to the smaller rooms of our own
wondering at size, at immensity where we sense
the shelter and have no sense of wall, where there seems
concern for us though no one there and we
feel thankful for what we give: our temporal
tininess and begin to love ourselves
as worthy deservers, as though we were ones who are loved
and go, bemused, back home. Alone there.

ENDINGS, THE END

I, remembering the false spring when
red-winged blackbirds cried assertive desire
in the bare elms and those elms dead by their look,
hear now, in August, cardinals cry, they
breeding again, I suppose.
                              It is summer still
but going to sleep, easy, my reflection is how
the end is not near, perhaps, but the end is sure:
desire is all, is its own end;
what else is to come?
                        I think how all our advance
is against each other—against, in the end, ourselves.
Whatever survives us we cannot recognize
though it may be—unknown—what we are
and we may be nothing and nothing lost when it comes
so all right, even so: we have to believe.

THE DISPOSITION

How one comes to question love—at least
to ourselves—and no one needs to hear us respond;
we aren't quite sure and we'd like the comfort of belief
even when we feel no comfort.
                                        It's easier
for some to say no and have it over but they
don't quite convince us or convince themselves.
                                              The strange

thing is our disposition—that where
we are isn't where we came to be: the place
is denied; we feel estranged there and begin
to build something homelier as though
we carried our place with us in a permanent mind
and fortified ourselves with new imaginings
that look like the old in a different place
and say we know better now and know how.

EVEN DON'T

When I was careful with coffee and otherwise
timorous: less liquor though not
abstaining, I may have improved. I lost some weight
soon recovered and hard to keep away.
Does it all matter? Why should I trouble you
with this? I think we bother ourselves with form
and extension, both soon gone and their worth
mistaken.
   We don't know the worth
of anything in spite of assertion.
       I'm glad
of my ignorance, that I don't need to know
and even what ignorance told me wasn't enough.
The sidelines is where I am, relieved
of those responsibilities we wish
we had. Use me, life, or even don't.

SOMEONE COMES BY

Come, Evil, into my house; the door
is open as it always was though not that you
were expected. But I should have known and perhaps
I did. No matter. You're here. What now? We have
to rearrange, I suppose and I don't know how.
You'll need a different name, not that you care
or care whatever adjustment I make. Sit down.
You're already at home. More than I am. We'll live.

UMPIRE

We don't have to know that the game score
is unimportant; we can go on thinking as if
it weren't or were. I don't care how big
we make the game—mondial or more,
say metaphysical—it's still play.
I can't think what else there is to do;
reality has left us out, neglects
to tell us even what goes on. Play ball!

CERTAIN QUESTIONS

The dreams are not happier—oh, far from that,
—some quite horrible—and still I prefer
them to the waking life except I'm not awake.
I'd dare to be; I've always wanted to know
—more maybe than anything else—what
it's about and the dreams seem closer to.
Are they though? That's what they don't say.

THE ACTION

It is confining to experience the world in acts.
We begin to think our acts are somehow the world:
all those people, narrative histories,
who felt what to whom and how and what
they did and what we did ourselves. Oh, no,
that isn't the world. I sit quiet, aware.
How very large the world is.

SOMETHING GOING ON

It is something like the weather—intentions unknown
to us, should it have intention and that unknown
also but we apparently none of its
intention, in no way its reference
but just the same happening to us,
its horrors and graces important as anything
—no, more important than anything—
that happens to us and it does happen to us
while we are busy with our own affairs as if
they mattered, thinking them real, watching them build
and prevail. They are brought to nothing: that isn't where
it's happening at all though we are there.

FRIENDS OF THE EARTH

Earth feels like home but it is after all
one of the planets of a star, in star terms,
nearby—no nearness to us. And Mars?
Venus? A planet is home? How could we think
of where we live—and it is where we live—in terms
we call human? God bless us! Something is wrong.
I can't put things together; atoms, too,
they have their distances, infinities
in respect of their smallnesses. Balks are built
into the system, balks are the base of it
—our system, our way to materialize.

STRUCTURAL STRESSES

Neither are the structures of dreams the way things are;
they serve to tell us how structures err in themselves
by being structures or simply to say that though
there may be structure somewhere, what we discern,
whether in sleep or awake, is never what is.

FORT EDWARD

When the train comes, I remember to lift my arm
and wave to the engineer. He smiles at me
and his hand waves back. His shiny tracks
recede to a distant point just as they should.
His various cars are firmly articulated.
The conductor checks his watch. The schedule is sure.

SHORT TERMS

It's one thing to learn the terms of the actual world
and make a kind of sense from that as though
the actual world exists—oh, we say it does,
our sense depends on it. Nonsense to pare
that. I do nonsensical things: how
should I speak about a world whose existence as world
I don't even claim and couldn't? For which I don't
have terms? I don't know; but it's where we are
if we need to say we are. I like it here.

A CONSOLATION OF COLD

Things don't move much in the winter; you
can go to bed early and expect, in the morning, to find
them right where you left them: a consolation of the cold
and we need it.
       Our lives are a strange
experience: I don't care how active we are in the world
it's still as though we never went out of the house
or got up in the morning, outside is where it goes on.

THE WINTER LIGHT

We see light but we live in the cold and the dark
—winters anyway. We are aware
that that isn't all that there is. We wouldn't have
it otherwise. How should we not know
and be alive, not be deprived? I saw
this afternoon the whiteness under the dark
clouds and rejoiced that we know the light as much
and even more from gone than when it is there.

PRESENT NOT ACCOUNTED FOR

We say the earth or the world made us among
the others, the still unnumbered multitude
of flowers, edible plants, the fishes and birds,
all fierce and fearful animals and gentle ones
—unhurried the earth or the world as if for forever—
or sun—say the sun whose strength afforded us
or say the process, itself, unstoppable
once started.
    We are accountants who make
our computations unfazed by infinite
intricacies of whatever mechanism
if it fixes accountability but these
are no more than another god brought out
of another machine and I say too easy an out.

WINTER EVENING

Cold hands in the afternoon then drink
and dinner. All I can think of is praise: its desire.

MANIFEST

There are no more problems and no more
solutions. There is only this hour whether it be
six or ten or twelve and nothing we
can do about it. We don't understand what it says
anyway. We let it see us as if it could see
or care as it probably doesn't and can't but then
neither do we or can. Well, we are here. OK.

THE INFORMER

What I think I mean is, against our death
our lives are nothing but become something when we think
of death. Temporality. We are here too short
to change things and anyway it isn't ours
to change. Our minds are directed otherwhere
by death. It comes up behind us to show us things.

END OF FEBRUARY

Bare ground now. The sun-mud
a shallow scum on the hard under. Walk
warily, it's grease. Through my clothes,
the sun adores me. Earth holds cold.

$$2 + 2 \, (= 1 ?)$$

Now, I want to say oh, God, yes
these impossible poems, crude and diverse:
what had you thought to say or didn't you think?
I guess I didn't nor planned them as a sequence. I took
them one at a time the way they came. Maybe they don't
add; we keep looking for whatever does.

ON SOME LINES FROM VIRGIL

"Respect the gods," Ilioneus is said
by Virgil to have said, "who are mindful of good
actions and of evil." This is translation, of course:
Virgil is Latin and Ilioneus,
I suppose, must have spoken Trojan but what
Trojan would have meant to Dido, whom he
addressed, is another matter. We often assume
a common language which doesn't exist
even in single countries. What should we make,
for example, of gods who are mindful of good
actions and of evil? Well, we know what he means
even though the terms are meaningless to us
(and may have been so to Ilioneus).
How can we say what we mean in terms we mean?

LUCIFER

Shun me. Adam's fall was trivial
to mine. I am too proud to contend His power,
will not be less and, as less, be least as known
beloved. Secret love is my desire.

ASTONISHMENT

It was perhaps not intended that we should speak,
in art, of transcendent values, assuming of course
intention by anyone or anything.
Unnecessary assumption: transcendence cares
nothing about intention whether or not.
But the things there are, you could say, assume we intend
them, have need of our tending. What does art declare
but the unintended discovered in what there is there
—an unexpected sum or product, a surprise
quotient or remainder, a value we hadn't thought
to look for, even, since we didn't know it implied
in any equation or any term of it?
We make our declarations in gratitude
for inordinacy of ordinary things.

SPORTSMONDAY
—or any other day—

I don't read the Sports Section, the real
sport is on the front page or in
the section called Business. I do
read that: I was there for thirty years
where I never did well at it but learned the terms
and still can laugh,—I used to not cry
and even was glad sometimes I didn't win
when I felt inadequate but that was a while ago.
I'm not sure we believe Sports are the game
there is but it's a comfort to think THEY PREPARE US FOR A WORLD
OF MEN and to think of the world of men in boys'
terms as though there were nothing else and go on
reading and playing Sports and PLAYING FOR REAL
and maybe they're right: it's the only game in town.

THE MOVIE

There is no need for it to make sense
or to make anything else. Whatever there is
to make has been made already and we catch
glimpses of it. Oh, we don't know
what it is and we could cry for that—we'd like
to know. We want the narrative but without,
there's scene after scene we wouldn't miss. We watch
entranced, wishing it all made sense sometime
as, of course, it doesn't. Well, maybe it will.

PERIOD METAPHOR

Jesus, spoke, metaphorically, about
houses built on rock and sand. I
don't have to use continental drift,
unheard of then, to challenge the metaphor
nor do I want to: I respect what
Jesus may have said, record be damned.
He must have said something I wish I believed
but, Jesus, God, there isn't any rock.

THE WORD

The Lord speaks to some and I don't ask
for certification nor do I envy them.
I question their hearing and go on, unspoken-to,
doing whatever the ignorant find to do.

THE LIFE

Hamlet suggested to Horatio a gap
in Horatio's life—commanded it really, "absent
thee from felicity," he said—to report
Hamlet's life. Hamlet was written, not
a writer but his writer knew: it's little enough
we know of Shakespeare's life or need to know—
he absented himself as Hamlet asked
Horatio to do. In some ways,
it's infelicitous: there isn't a life
—if that's what we want—of our own to be
reported. There's only life and it isn't ours.
I wonder why both Auden and Eliot
wanted papers burned or unrecorded?
They must have known how they were absent too
and how little it mattered. Does somebody care?
Let the little be known and let it be plain
life isn't about us; it's about
itself and that's what we try to write about:
the light it makes of us to see it by
and the iterate, pitiless deaths it needs to show.

THE AGE OF SCIENCE

Proven truth is something for everyman
Except for the ones who won't listen, won't learn.
We can show them but we can't make them believe
—that wouldn't be rational anyway and we don't
try. Admittedly, we don't have
the whole thing; that's what our method's about
but, at least, we have a method at last and if
it doesn't work I don't know what we can do.

THE POWERS OF NUMBERS

Are we one or are we two? Thinking of one, we think of an all without division or we think of a thing set distinctly apart, a denial of unity other than unity as an aggregation of distinct parts not really one, an enormous sum of uniquenesses. In such a huge aggregation, two is insignificant in any serious counting: impossible to reach the others that way. Two is not one added to one but one which is split and made one again; it is a denial of one as an apartness, a division devised to make or make again a unity.

The question of one or two is an internal question. It asks whether we first need to divide to make one. The concept of two disregards any aggregation of uniquenesses, dismisses the existence of it. If it says two it says two in order to assert one. Why then two? Something about one seems to think two necessary as perhaps it is. Maybe, in order to seem to be. It is in the dualism of either and or that oneness discovers itself, that the indefinite is defined, that duality makes unities. In opposition, what had been vague comes clear as much as though it existed only then.

If one demands two and is equal to it and has that single equality despite greater sums and more complex ones, then those greater complexities are incomplete and partial. Two rightly disregards them. And if, again, we allow them and their validity, we see how little they, conversely, make of two: however close two may be to one it is still near to nothing.

I wake in the morning and look outside; there may be something there. One added to one is still one. It doesn't make two. Two is an otherness, a division, a fractioning of one. It is an uneasy relationship always carrying, as it does, that slant line of division which is, at once, its mark and its instability. Two is a unit but a divided unit.

One instability of the division that makes two from one is that the division, once made, may be made again by one or the other and be repeated indefinitely. Two is dismissed. In that fraction, moreover, which is two's division and juncture there is often a wide disproportion of the parts. This disproportion would sometimes seem to be what holds it together. A full equality doubles the divider to an equals sign and, by canceling otherness, makes simple unities or a standoff. A very large numerator may ask that several whole numbers first be factored out. One thinks of fortuitous and seemingly fortunate cases as, say, twenty-four over five which after successive factoring-outs of four fives is seen to reach the closeness of four fifths. More often maybe one sees the opposite times when the numerator is much the smaller figure asserting however its claim slight enough to leave the denominator almost free; but that claim is the cause of the fraction, its stabilizer.

If one means to go on to even greater numbers there is a sense, of course, in which two is greater than one; but in the fractioning of one to make a unitary two something is always necessarily left out and, as a result, the fraction is not more than one but less. The integer is universal.

The person is not an integer; individuals are divided and if this is so in surgery and reproduction, how much more is it so of the mind and of the whole self far though it be from the whole. We speak of self but even the selfish person lives in a world of outside terms, disputing numbers. It is as though our living has little to do with us and concerns itself, not with self, but with certain abstractions, numbers among them, and the shapes abstractions take in dreams, the contentions they make, is what we are, even awake. Viral, they command for their continuance the cells themselves of our bodies.

THE I'S AND EARS OF THE WORLD

Happiness is not to be achieved;
it is to be attended as one among
all the strangenesses we are asked to hear.
Not goals but sound is for listeners.

HOW ELSE?

How we feel about it can be altered by
money or alcohol—other things—
and this is to say that how we feel about
it hasn't much to do with what it is.

But no, since we don't know anyway
what it is, I suppose we have to go
on how we feel about it knowing that
we'll never, in any way, know what it is.

What I find too easy is the adjustment I make to accept.

MANNER OF SPEAKING

So much of what we say is, as we say,
a way to say it. Those not content with that
may begin to believe what is said. Even, at times,
the speakers do. Better is what they should know.

AND FURTHERMORE

AURA

Their emanations have not been specified
but there are rays not x
nor gamma nor infra-red—what else?
At times, the beautifully empty or seemingly
empty sky, blue with a few clouds,
is filled with them: the glory of the world.

PLENARY INDULGENCE

I give the body what it wants: sweets
and caresses, fatty substances, firm
beds to support it. Oh, I could refuse
for whatever reasons; they make their cases, some
persuasively on the body's side as to say
what's good for the body despite its wants and I know
the body will, someday, fail me, will anyway
in the end and the spirit wants a body to love.

NOLO CONTENDERE

Should our occasional conceptions save
us? I think of mine as some but also think
of those thought better of. We might, I suppose,
be merciful and patient. We try; who
should condemn us? We do the best we can
and it's nothing—or no, not nothing but
miles away from the unlived life.
Our failures want our erasure; let it come.

SO LONG

A black hole may lie at the center of our
galaxy which is not the center of anything else
I guess but even so. It's a heaviness
notable in a massy universe
because so small for so much mass. Some
people think the universe is full of spots
of heaviness much tinier
than this which relieve problems about the weight
of the universe. In a sense, black holes
are an emptiness in their mass: nothing there
to be seen and nothing coming out—well,
maybe something. We ought to know soon
and I should wait until we know before
I talk. Ah well, I should live so long.

FOLLY

We love the land the way we love ourselves
and love each other: we kill and die. Do we want
this? I suppose we must, default of a way
different and we don't know of one of the same
depth. Milder ways don't work
though my mind seizes on them, wishes they might.
I want less than the folly of the world.
I love what is wasted, don't yield the way.

SOME WHERE

The visible in materialization is not
the material but the energy behind
or under it or within. Somewhere;
who knows? It isn't the material we take
it to be. This is a sadness: if it were, it were more
accessible. Well, maybe it shouldn't be,
as it isn't, certainly and we learn from that
that the material is nothing, is unpossessed
because nothing there to take or not what we want
anyway. Our energy wants
its energy and both of us material
—as the universe, say, what we see of it:
we want its matter real and we a part
of it—a material someone somewhere.

MORTAL LOVES

My last elm is gone and I had many.
Oh, there are seedlings: little trees come up
and live for awhile as though they expected life
to last forever. Well, it doesn't—at least
not theirs. Or ours either. I
don't think it will nor do I want it to.
Love acknowledges it lives in time.

THE PUNCHBOARD

We die quite randomly of various
diseases—and early—though not so early as once.
Medically, that change is understandable
but the fact itself is still there—may
reassert itself. The full life we think
of (and what *do* we think of it?) is not
really the norm. It isn't not normal
to be brief and strange: we needn't reckon with that
and we don't but, however we think or say, we know.

THE UNTOLD

Water goes softly into the air and comes
again as the water it always was and, with sleep,
our waking goes in and out, alert, aware,
listening for what it may overhear.

OXYMORONIC FUNDAMENT

The woods at the edge of the lawn puzzles me.
I don't understand the ways of its complex
branches: how they hold me. I watch as lights
vary; they don't advance me in any way,
are indifferent to me—I could cut them down.
The nothing I hear is still talk, a part
of their presence, unlearned, a vestige of silence which
preceded them, was content unspoken and is said.

GUIDED TOUR

I am sorry to disappoint you and I know
you expected a lot more but the distances
of the universe are right here. You
wanted mysteries which could be explained,
made understandable as your disappointment is,
I know because I, too, am embarrassed to say
it's no more than this which is just what we knew
since we knew anything. Well, take a look.

KNOWLEDGE OF PLATES

Earth and rocks of the earth used to be
our metaphor for unchanging—little we knew.
Knowing may well be our error—I as much
as anyone. Not that I know but I
wanted to. I still do; we like
to act as if there were certainties,
as if we could learn. Well, a few things we can.

ALTERNATIVE

If we are reality and I hesitate
to say we are, then the strength of reality
finds us willing and indistinct, uses us
as part of its own horror, its able arm.
Otherwise, I should think we could rectify.

METAPHOR AGAIN

Oh, make a world, OK
but its glory will go and the stones it's built on
will erode and frost-fracture or something else
in warmer climates. Never mind what else
would make the metaphor; the world is one
itself and not to be taken word for word
any more than other metaphors:
pronouncements, dogmas, ideologies,
hard facts, material truth. Give up
and believe without, say praise, give thanks.

OUTSIDE

Oh, we know what goes on or someone will give
us the real dirt. Quite a few were there
at the cabinet table or in the locker room
and heard direct. They know what was said and where
the power was. Not that someone else
—and he might have his reasons—also there
might not tell us different and be right but then
it isn't simple and keeps us occupied
not just with now but with ancient history
while elsewhere it happens if happens is what it does
and I don't think so and I don't know what goes on.

THE IDEA OF REAL

This can't be the real world and to put the two
words together defines the problem or poses it:
can worlds be real? Can we know reality?
Reality of the world is what we say
it is and we can be wrong limitless times
and try it again. All right; we have a sense
of real. It moves us. Maybe real is.

HOLY ORDERS

What counts is that we write it down or paint,
dance, compose, the way we are given to.
So watch and hear and the hell with what we thought
it should do: it doesn't care about us.

ESTRANGEMENT

One way I think we don't exist
is that we would be such a strange thing
for it to use. What a strange thing it is.

ANYWAY

I want to cry my wild happiness
—wild because it hasn't anything
to do with the cultivated ways: not sex
or Zen or Jesus or even as though
I thought that happiness was a place to look.
It wasn't and I didn't and here it is.

FOR GIL, COWORKER

Your new book came today and I was urged
to read what I may no more like than one
of my poems which I may detest at first and be right
to do so as if there were standards we understand
our work had to meet and we went about to do that.
We don't. We write whatever we have to write.

FORESIGHT

I lie in bed
practicing dead;
it may take some
getting used to.

RUINED PLACE

Ruined place: it was all magnificence
from what little there is to be seen: a noble arm,
broken pieces, paving stones.
                          The wall
was here and this wide space from what
was a gate, the principal street leading to a kind
of citadel at the end where the mound is.
We know there were buildings on either side. Some bones
have been found from which we know the date
approximately but not what place it was.
Maybe it doesn't matter: we know there have been
lots of places lost in the world. It's what
it's about and we know how men are driven to wars
and violences that, to our waking life,
bring home the sweetness that horror has in dreams.

EATING ALONE

I don't set a place for Elijah at my table but there's room
and food and, if he should come, he's welcome here.

FOR MY FRIEND, JERRY, HE DRUNK

Yes, but there's something more than
the rational life and it asks us kill
me, kill yourself, kill the life where you are;
There's life and a better one on the other side.
You want this shit? You can have it: be good.
And even if there's not another life . . . this?

God give me love; it's what I have.

STAND-BY

Nobody wants to die—well, almost none.
And we all dread the waiting around, the delayed
departure, empty time, nothing to do.

The time comes we've seen it and aren't sure
—is it it? Maybe there's more and even if not
what should we do? We wait anyway.

ETIQUETTE

When the body is sovereign
—its desire—
(we say the body)
well all right
the body is sovereign
—its desire—

but the times it isn't
it can be gracious
and we are courteous
in its dismissal.

FINDING THE WAY

Who needs a way? The point is there isn't one
except, of course, yes, the way is out.
We are stupid and dirty but stay with us.

STATIONS

The metaphor of the cross however it once
was positioned or temporized gives us a place
and time as though it had a specific one.

Oh, God, I sense it is now and wherever.
                                    Slight
and momentary, I bear the pain with you.

Redemption is not possible because
we are all part of it and no one there
to be redeemed.
                    You mean the empty ones too
who don't know or feel?
                    Yes, I mean them.
Sufferer, your goodness, oh God, is in
your torment and compulsion.
                    I will have no other God.

THE END OF THE WORLD

Losses anyway—terrible
losses. Who cares if final ones?
It wasn't our idea: we came to it.

GETTING OLDER

When I was young I didn't drink alcohol.
Well, yes, I did but I didn't drink much. I went
for days and weeks without it—money partly
I guess—but I didn't think in those terms as such
because everything is money when you haven't it
and it isn't a particular term; it's just part
of the basics.
         Now, I don't remember what
it was I started to say but that may be age
and have nothing at all to do with alcohol.

MORE OR LESS

A definition of desire is not to say
what satisfies me : less
than that does. It is to say what
is unsayable, what doesn't satisfy.

Design by David Bullen
Typeset in Mergenthaler Imprint
by Wilsted & Taylor
Printed by Malloy Lithographing
on acid-free paper